Jacqueline Bouvier Kennedy Onassis

Jacqueline Bouvier Kennedy Onassis

✶✶✶✶✶✶✶✶✶✶✶✶✶✶✶✶✶✶✶✶

1929–1994

BY DAN SANTOW

CHILDREN'S PRESS®
A Division of Grolier Publishing
New York London Hong Kong Sydney
Danbury, Connecticut

Consultants:	CARL SFERRAZZA ANTHONY *Historical researcher and author of* First Ladies: The Saga of the Presidents' Wives and Their Power; *historical consultant to the* *Smithsonian Institution's First Ladies exhibit* LINDA CORNWELL *Learning Resource Consultant* *Indiana Department of Education*
Project Editor: Page Layout: Photo Researcher:	DOWNING PUBLISHING SERVICES CAROLE DESNOES JAN IZZO

Visit Children's Press on the Internet at:
http://publishing.grolier.com

Library of Congress Cataloging-in-Publication Data
Santow, Dan.
    Jacqueline Bouvier Kennedy Onassis / by Dan Santow.
        p.   cm. — (Encyclopedia of first ladies)
    Includes bibliographical references and index.
    Summary: Presents a biography of the wife of the thirty-fifth president of the United
States, an elegant and fashionable First Lady who helped Washington become the social
and cultural center of the country.
    ISBN 0-516-20477-7
    1. Onassis, Jacqueline Kennedy, 1929–1994—Juvenile literature. 2. Presidents'
spouses—United States—Biography—Juvenile literature. 3. Celebrities—United States—
Biography—Juvenile literature. [1. Onassis, Jacqueline Kennedy, 1929–1994. 2. First ladies.
3. Women—Biography.] I. Title. II. Series.
CT275.0552S26   1998
973.922'092—dc21   97-47280
[B]   CIP
                                              AC

Table of Contents

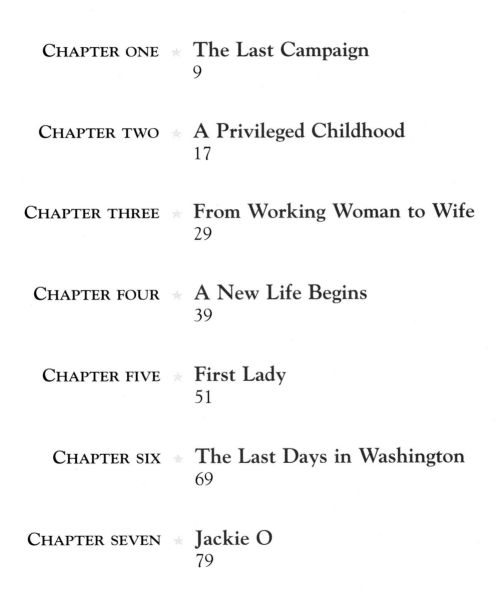

Jacqueline Bouvier Kennedy Onassis

CHAPTER ONE

The Last Campaign

☆ ☆ ☆ ☆ ☆ ☆ ☆ ☆ ☆ ☆ ☆ ☆ ☆ ☆ ☆ ☆

By the time November 1963 rolled around, it had been nearly a year since First Lady Jacqueline Kennedy had accompanied her husband, President John F. Kennedy, on any official outings.

In August, she had given birth to a a son, Patrick Bouvier. The premature baby died of heart failure less than two days later. Jacqueline had stayed at the Kennedy summer home, then traveled to Greece and Turkey with her sister. It had been a shock, of course, when the child she and the president wanted so very badly died. But she was able to take comfort in her two remaining children, six-year-old Caroline and two-

☆ ☆ ☆ ☆ ☆ ☆ ☆ ☆ ☆ ☆ ☆ ☆ ☆ ☆ ☆ ☆

The Kennedys are shown here with Governor John Connally and his wife in San Antonio, the first stop on the Kennedy's campaign trip to Texas.

year-old John Jr., both of whom she loved very much.

The president's reelection campaign was starting to gear up. Knowing that he needed to rally support in the state of Texas, Jacqueline agreed to go with her husband for a three-day visit. The trip was to be capped off with a few days of relaxation and horseback riding at Vice President Lyndon Johnson and Lady Bird Johnson's ranch outside the state capital of Austin.

JFK and Civil Rights

✴ ✴ ✴ ✴ ✴ ✴ ✴ ✴ ✴ ✴ ✴ ✴ ✴ ✴ ✴ ✴ ✴ ✴ ✴ ✴

During John Kennedy's brief presidency, African Americans spoke out loudly for equality. In the South especially, public places, buses, schools, and restrooms were still segregated. Whites discouraged blacks from voting and discriminated against them in the workplace. Groups demanding civil rights marched and demonstrated, often facing violent mobs. Although he believed in equality for all Americans, Kennedy reacted cautiously to the growing discontent. Finally, in 1963, moved by the determination of the young civil-rights leader Martin Luther King Jr., Kennedy sponsored the long-awaited legislation to give blacks equal access to all public places and to strengthen their voting rights. Although many people felt that Kennedy's response was too little and came too late, he had timed it to make sure that it would pass through Congress. Sadly, President Kennedy did not live to see the Civil Rights Act pass in 1964.

President Kennedy addressed a breakfast meeting in Fort Worth on the morning of November 22, 1963, just before the trip to Dallas.

a breakfast meeting the next morning. Jackie, as she was known to all the world, was late arriving at the meeting. The crowd, many of whom had attended just to get a peek at the woman who was always at the top of every "best dressed" and "most admired" list, was anxious. "Mrs. Kennedy is busy organizing herself," the president said with his typical wit and charm. "It takes a little longer

Early on November 21, the First Lady and the president flew to Texas—first to San Antonio, where he dedicated a new medical center, and then to Houston, for a fund-raising dinner. There, Jacqueline spoke in Spanish to a Mexican group. Later that night, the couple flew to Fort Worth, where the president addressed

When the Kennedys arrived in Dallas, Jackie was given a huge bouquet of red roses.

11

Lyndon Baines Johnson (1908–1973)

★ ★

Lyndon Johnson taking the oath of office just after the death of President John F. Kennedy

When this strapping Texan was thrust into the presidency by John Kennedy's death in 1963, he was ready to rise to the challenge. He had tried to run for president in 1960, but Kennedy won the nomination and Johnson settled for his invitation to run as vice president. A lifelong politician, Johnson's experience as a Senate leader served him well. Although his down-home style was very different from Kennedy's social polish, Johnson had incredible energy and determination. His keen understanding of government allowed him to push Kennedy's civil-rights bills through Congress. Johnson won his own election in 1964, promoting civil rights, health care, and educational programs as part of his "Great Society." His final undoing, however, would be the Vietnam War, which dragged on endlessly. In 1968, he declined to run for president again.

you know, but then she looks so much better than we do!"

There was still one city to go—Dallas—where they were greeted by 5,000 well-wishers. Jackie was given a bouquet of red roses, which offset the pink suit and hat the president had specially chosen for her to wear. Jack and Jackie climbed into the back seat of a long, black convertible for the ride to the Dallas Trade Mart, where the president was to give a speech. With them were Texas Governor John Connally and his wife. The vice

The Kennedys and Connallys rode in the same long, black convertible in the Dallas motorcade.

president and Mrs. Johnson rode in another car. Jackie placed the roses on the seat next to her and off they went. It was a glorious day—warm and cloudless. Crowds lined the streets.

"You can't say Dallas doesn't love you, Mr. President," the governor's wife said to him.

"You sure can't," he responded, smiling.

Jackie was waving to the crowd on her left while Jack was waving to the crowd on his right. Suddenly, just as they passed a building called the Texas

School Book Depository, three ear-splitting shots rang out. Jackie turned toward the president, who was clutching his throat. He had been hit in the neck, head, and throat by the bullets. There was blood everywhere.

"Oh my God," Jackie screamed, as his limp body slumped against her shoulder, "they've killed my husband! Jack! Jack!"

It had happened so fast and so unexpectedly that she didn't know what to do or where to turn. Without thinking, she began to seek help by crawl-

President Kennedy slumped over in the car after being hit by an assassin's bullets.

ing out of her seat and over the back of the trunk. But the car began to careen toward the hospital at 75 miles per hour. All she could do was hold his body until they reached the hospital nine minutes later.

As the doctors feverishly tried to save the president's life, Jackie stood by watching.

"I want to be there when he dies," she told the nurse. Later, when she found out that it was a disgruntled citizen who had assassinated the president, Jackie became even more miserable, if that were possible. "He didn't even have the satisfaction of being killed for civil rights," she lamented,

knowing that her husband had been proud of his fight for equality for all people.

By two o'clock that afternoon, on a day that had started out so perfectly, Jackie was back on the plane returning to Washington, D.C. Her husband's body lay in a coffin nearby. When Lady Bird Johnson, wife of the new president, asked if she wanted to change her blood-soaked clothes before landing, she said no.

"I want them to see what they've done to Jack," Jackie told her.

Though she knew that her official duties as First Lady were over forever, she also knew that she had one last

Presidential Assassinations

✶ ✶

President Abraham Lincoln was asssassinated by John Wilkes Booth at Ford's Theatre.

Including John F. Kennedy, four American presidents have been assassinated (or murdered) in office. Just after the Civil War ended, Southern loyalist John Wilkes Booth shot Abraham Lincoln on April 14, 1864, as he sat in a theater box enjoying a play. Lincoln died the following day. In 1881, Charles Guiteau, a deranged and disappointed office-seeker, wounded President James Garfield in a Washington railroad station. Garfield lingered for more than two months, unable to serve as president. While visiting the Pan-American Exposition in Buffalo in 1901, President William McKinley was gunned down by political terrorist Leon Czolgosz. McKinley died eight days later. Unlike these men, no modern president would dream of appearing in public without ample protection. Increased security has foiled recent attempts on presidential lives—including attacks on Presidents Ford and Reagan.

important act to perform. That was to plan the president's funeral. It had to be solemn, of course, but grand, too, and memorable. Her husband, after all, had been president of the United States, the most powerful man in the world. In the opinion of many, he had changed that world for the better.

✶ ✶ ✶ ✶ ✶ ✶ ✶ ✶ ✶ ✶ ✶ ✶ ✶ ✶ ✶

CHAPTER TWO

A Privileged Childhood

Jacqueline Bouvier was born into a well-to-do family in Southhampton, New York. Her mother, Janet, was only twenty-one years old when she gave birth to Jackie on July 28, 1929. Her father, Jack, was thirty-seven, a stockbroker who also had come from a wealthy family. He was determined to raise Jackie and her younger sister Lee in the same fashion in which he had been raised. The family lived in New York City in a grand Park Avenue apartment, complete with a maid, a nanny, and a cook. Jackie took ballet and piano lessons and spent time at the family's large summer cottage on the shore.

Jackie was known to be an intelligent child. She was talking by her first birthday and made her first public appearance when she was two. On that occasion, she showed her dog at a dog show.

A young Jacqueline Lee Bouvier with her dog

of Ernest Hemingway, F. Scott Fitzgerald, and Edith Wharton. Louis Armstrong wailed on his trumpet and nightclubs pulsed with the rhythms of jazz. In New York, the Museum of Modern Art opened, and in Los Angeles, the first Oscars were awarded for cinematic excellence. And, for the first time ever, Americans could travel between those two cities in a grueling 48 hours: flying by day and taking the train by night.

Baseball fans adored "The Bambino" (George Herman "Babe" Ruth), the New York Yankee who hit his 500th home run in 1929. But most of all, Americans loved their radios and their cars. Radio, only about nine years old, boasted 618 stations coast to coast in 1929. Nearly 14 million households tuned in nightly to programs of music and variety. Car making became the leading American industry in 1929, when 3 million automobiles were produced. No wonder Motorola soon began making the first car radios.

The Roaring Twenties came to a screeching halt, however, on October 29, known grimly as "Black Tuesday." That day, the stock market suffered the most disastrous losses in its history, ruining American investors and triggering the Great Depression of the 1930s.

Her mother, who was an accomplished horsewoman, gave Jackie riding lessons. She took naturally to them and at a very early age was riding alone, even competing and winning.

Though it took a certain amount of discipline to learn to ride, Jackie had her mischievous side, too. Once, when Jackie was four years old, she wandered away from her nanny while playing in Central Park. She was found by a police officer. He brought her to the station and called her mother. When her mother arrived to fetch little Jackie, her daughter was chatting amiably with the policeman. Janet asked what had happened. Jackie had walked up to him in the park, he told her mother, and stated, "My nurse is lost!"

This 1935 photo shows Jackie at the age of six riding with her mother.

Jackie became an excellent horsewoman at a very young age. She is shown here with her father just after she had won a ribbon in a riding competition.

As a girl, Jackie attended Chapin School in New York City.

New York, U.S.A.

✫ ✫

Jacqueline Bouvier was born in New York, the Empire State, in 1929. New York stretches from the Atlantic Ocean west to the Great Lakes and north to Canada. The great metropolis of New York City occupies its southernmost corner, while lovely farm and forestlands cover most of its 49,000 square miles (127,000 km²). It became the eleventh state in 1788, and its capital was established at Albany in 1797. In 1929, New York had more people than any other state in the Union, and half of them (or their parents) had been born overseas. Huge numbers of Europeans had come to the United States seeking better lives since 1880, many of them settling in New York State. Another group of newcomers—black people from America's South—came to New York in great numbers during the 1920s. They settled in Harlem on the northern end of Manhattan Island in New York City and made it the country's center of African-American culture.

That sort of sassiness stayed with her throughout her childhood. She was nothing if not honest. When she and Lee were in their apartment's elevator one day, Lee looked at the elevator man and complimented his crest of blond hair. "Ernest, you look very pretty today," she told him. Jackie looked at him, too, and then turned to Lee.

"How can you say such a thing, Lee? It isn't true. You know perfectly well that Ernest looks just like a rooster!"

At Chapin, the private school she attended in New York, Jackie always got good grades. She loved to read *Winnie the Pooh*, *The Wizard of Oz*, and *Peter Rabbit*. Even though she got good grades, she also got into trouble

A Tale of Two Sisters

★ ★ ★ ★ ★ ★ ★ ★ ★ ★ ★ ★ ★ ★ ★ ★ ★ ★ ★ ★

The two Bouvier sisters lived charmed yet bittersweet lives. While Jackie grew up to be a president's wife, her younger sister Lee became a princess. In 1959, when

she was twenty-six, Lee married Prince Stanislas Radziwill, a Polish nobleman who had become an English citizen. The prince was twenty years older than Lee and very rich. The couple divided their time among an elegant London town house near Buckingham Palace, a country estate, and an apartment in New York. They had two children, Antony and Anna. Lee built a reputation for interior decoration and tried her hand at acting. All the while, Jackie and Lee remained close, often traveling together. Lee's marriage to the prince ended in divorce in 1974, and he died two years later. Today, Lee owns a store in New York City.

with the principal, Miss Stringfellow. In fact, Jackie misbehaved in school so much that once when her mother asked her what happened when she was sent to the principal's office, Jackie said, "Well, I go into her office and Miss Stringfellow says, 'Jacqueline, sit down. I've heard bad reports about you.' I sit down. Then Miss Stringfellow says a lot of things. But I don't listen."

Eventually, Miss Stringfellow had had enough. Jackie was a smart girl but unruly. Because Jackie loved horses so much, Miss Stringfellow thought that she could explain to her why she needed to behave well, using a horse as an example. Jackie was like a horse in certain ways, Miss Stringfellow told her. "You can run fast. You have staying power. You're well-built and you have brains. But if you're not properly broke and trained, you'll be good for nothing. Suppose you owned the most beautiful racehorse in the world. What good would it be if he weren't trained to stay on the track, to stand still at the starting gate, to obey commands? He couldn't even pull a milk truck or a trash cart. He would be use-

Jackie at Belmont Race Track in 1939, when she was ten years old.

less to you and you would have to get rid of him." It was an invaluable lesson, one that stayed with Jackie for the rest of her life.

But not everything in young Jackie's life was rosy. Her parents fought often. When they argued, Jackie and her sister often stood in the hall and listened.

When Jackie was fourteen years old, her mother married Hugh Auchincloss and moved to Merrywood, his estate in McLean, Virginia.

At fifteen, Jackie entered Miss Porter's School in Connecticut.

Jackie (holding reins) and her friends at Miss Porter's School enjoyed winter sleigh rides.

When she was ten years old, the Bouviers divorced. Jackie and seven-year-old Lee split their time between their mother and father. During the week, while they were with their mother, the girls had chores to do, homework to complete, and after-school lessons to take. When they were with their father, it seemed to be all fun. He would take Jackie to fancy restaurants, buy her expensive clothes, and take her on vacations to the beach. Once, he even rented a puppy for her to walk through Central Park!

When Jackie turned fourteen, her mother remarried another very wealthy man, Hugh D. Auchincloss. The family moved to his ivy-covered estate outside Washington, D.C.

The following year, Jackie went off to a boarding school in Connecticut called Miss Porter's School. Though Jackie was very popular with the boys from nearby prep schools, she had many interests—in and out of school. She excelled at art, history, English, and literature. She collected books and took care of her horse Danseuse,

JACQUELINE LEE BOUVIER
"MERRYWOOD"
MC LEAN, VIRGINIA
"Jackie"

Favorite Song: Lime House Blues
Always Saying: "Play a Rhumba next"
Most Known For: Wit
Aversion: People who ask if her horse is still alive
Where Found: Laughing with Tucky
Ambition: Not to be a house-wife

Jackie's senior yearbook picture

who was stabled on campus. "Danseuse was a family horse and every child had a ride on her," Jackie once wrote. "She was such a lady. She flicked her tiny feet out in front of her when she trotted. There was a soft pink spot on the end of her nose and she would snuffle softly when she knew you had an apple for her." Jackie wrote short stories and poems and contributed articles and cartoons to the school newspaper.

In her senior yearbook under ambition, she wrote: "Not to be a house-wife."

When Jackie entered Vassar College in Poughkeepsie, New York, she studied the history of religion, Shakespeare, and literature. She learned to speak Spanish, Italian, and French. During her junior year, she went to Paris to study at the Sorbonne. She loved big-city life in Paris and learning about French art

Bicycles were a popular mode of transportation on the Vassar College campus.

and literature. When she returned to the United States, the thought of returning to Vassar's country setting didn't appeal to her. She transferred to George Washington University in Washington, D.C.

Her love of France stayed with her, and she had always had an interest in fashion. When *Vogue* magazine offered a contest—the first prize being a job with the magazine in Paris and then in their New York offices—Jackie jumped at the chance to enter.

She wrote an essay on "People I Wish I Had Known," and included Charles Baudelaire, a famous French poet, and Oscar Wilde, an English writer. She wrote that they were both "idealists who could paint sinfulness with honesty and still believe in something higher. . . . Both were rich men's sons who lived like dandies, ran through what they had, and died in extreme poverty." Jackie won the contest, but the decision to leave her family again was difficult. Eventually, she decided to stay in the capital and look for work.

★ ★ ★ ★ ★ ★ ★ ★ ★ ★ ★ ★ ★ ★ ★

CHAPTER THREE

From Working Woman to Wife

* * * * * * * * * * * * * * * * *

S ince she had written for her school newspapers
and had won the *Vogue* contest, Jackie was sure
that she wanted to go into journalism. She applied for
a job with the *Washington Times–Herald.*

"Do you really want to work here," the editor asked
her, "or do you want to hang around here until you get
married?" Jackie looked him straight in the eye and
said, "No sir. I want to make a career!" With that, he
hired her as an inquiring reporter. She was paid $42.50
a week to go around and ask people on the street—
congressmen, judges, and whomever else she could
find—witty and interesting questions. She would

* * * * * * * * * * * * * * * * *

Not Home Alone

✶ ✶

Although John Kennedy's time as president was short, it linked two very different eras for American women. The 1950s were years of tremendous prosperity in the United States. Americans had suffered through the depression of the 1930s and World War II in the 1940s. They were now ready for the good life. They bought homes in the suburbs, automobiles, and appliances. And they began to have more children. Women who had held jobs during the war returned to homemaking, while men commuted to jobs in the city to support their wives and children. Family togetherness in a spacious suburban home seemed to be everyone's dream.

Despite appearances, however, changes were taking place among America's women. During the 1950s, more women entered college than ever before. Between 1940 and 1960, the number of working wives doubled as families realized that it would take two incomes to be able to afford the good life. Women could not earn as much as men, however, and most still worked as typists, nurses, or teachers. The opportunities for female lawyers and doctors were few. So, even though more women were working outside the home as the 1960s dawned, they began to feel frustrated by their limited opportunities. They began to demonstrate for equal rights. Feminism and women's liberation movements grew strong. Soon, American women who wanted professional lives would never again be limited to finding happiness in the home alone.

record their answer and take their picture. It was 1951 and they called her the Inquiring Photographer.

One night, she attended a dinner party at a friend's house. There, she met a handsome young congressman from Massachusetts named John Fitzgerald Kennedy. Jackie was twenty-two years old; Jack, as he was called, was thirty-four. They began to date and became a popular, glamorous couple around town. Jackie's life

Jackie at work at the Washington Times–Herald

encompassed more than just an endless round of parties, however. She translated books on politics from French into English for Jack, and helped to write his speeches. When Jackie was in London covering the coronation of Queen Elizabeth in May 1953, Jack proposed to her over the phone. There was a lot of static on the line, but she had heard the question clearly enough to immediately agree to his proposal.

Jackie and Jack playing tennis during the summer before their wedding

Sailing was a favorite pastime for Jack and Jackie before and after their marriage.

Fit for a Queen

☆ ☆

Reporting on Queen Elizabeth's coronation, the ceremony that promoted her from princess to queen, Jacqueline must have been impressed by such wonders as the State Coach. Nearly 200 years old at that time, the carved and gilded carriage is used only for coronations. Her Majesty wore a gown of white satin embroidered with the emblem of Great Britain. All the nobles of England and nobility from around the world gathered in Westminster Abbey to see the queen crowned. And what a crown! The Archbishop of Canterbury placed the deep red, jewel-encircled St. Edward's Crown on her head. Worn only at coronations, it was so heavy that Elizabeth traded it for the lighter Imperial Crown halfway through the ceremony.

Their storybook-perfect wedding took place that autumn in Newport, Rhode Island, where her stepfather had a large country house called Hammersmith Farm. There were 600 guests at the church service and more than 1,000 at the luncheon that followed. Jackie wore a pale, cream-colored gown. Her bridesmaids wore pale pink dresses with burgundy sashes and

Jack and Jackie's wedding reception was held at Hammersmith Farm (left), the large country house in Newport, Rhode Island, that was owned by Jackie's stepfather.

Archbishop Richard Cushing presided over the Kennedy's marriage ceremony, which took place at St. Mary's Church in Newport.

The bride and groom just after their wedding

The Kennedys honeymooned in Acapulco, Mexico.

tiny hats. She and Jack spent their honeymoon in a pink cottage overlooking the sea in Acapulco, Mexico.

It was the start of what would be a difficult but loving marriage for them both. Though they loved one another and shared much in common, from their love of great books to their love of sailing, they also had their differences. Jackie was an intensely private person, and though she herself had been a newspaper reporter, she did not care much for the press. (Once, when she was asked what she was going to feed her new puppy, she answered, "Reporters.")

Jack, however, loved the limelight. He was a politician, after all, and enjoyed giving speeches before huge crowds, wading into the sidelines to shake hands and hold babies. Jackie knew she would have to make certain accommodations in her new role. And Jack knew that the same stubbornness for which she had been known as a little girl was still part of her.

On the day of their wedding, at least, no one knew if theirs was a good match or not. "The bride's mother," Jack once kiddingly wrote to a friend, "has a tendency to think I am not good enough for her daughter!"

☆ ☆ ☆ ☆ ☆ ☆ ☆ ☆ ☆ ☆ ☆ ☆ ☆ ☆ ☆

CHAPTER FOUR

A New Life Begins

It was freezing cold in the nation's capital on January 20, 1961. The night before, a huge storm had blanketed the city with 8 inches (20 centimeters) of snow. It was windy, icy, and difficult to get around. But it was Inauguration Day, the day John F. Kennedy was being sworn in as the thirty-fifth president of the United States. "Ask not what your country can do for you," he said in his speech to the nation. "Ask what you can do for your country."

Jack and Jackie had been married for seven years, and it had taken a lot of hard work to win the presidential election.

Jack Kennedy accepting his nomination as the Democratic party's presidential candidate in the 1960 election

During the presidential campaign, Jackie wrote a series of columns called "Campaign Wife."

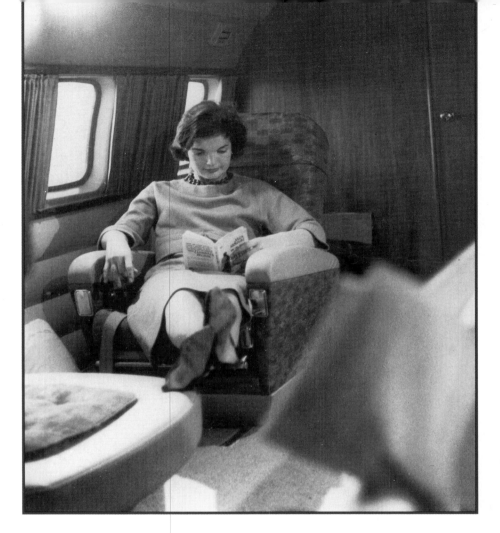

Jackie on a plane in April 1960 on her way to the next campaign stop.

Jackie enjoyed campaigning, especially when she could talk about Jack's record. Once, during the presidential primaries, she was in a grocery store and picked up a microphone to announce, "Just keep on with your shopping while I tell you about my husband, John F. Kennedy!" Jack began to see his wife not just as a pretty thing but as a helpmate, as someone on whom he could rely and trust. "As usual, Jackie's drawing more people than we are," he told an aide after one appearance.

Though she often accompanied her husband on the campaign trail,

The Kennedys at Idlewild Airport during the 1960 presidential campaign

Jackie preferred not to do too much campaigning on her own. And Jack had understood. She had suffered a miscarriage in 1955 and had a still-born child in 1956, which had been a great disappointment to them both. In 1957, she gave birth to Caroline, who was now three. Jackie intended to spend as much time with her daughter as possible.

Still, she did campaign once in a while. In Worcester, Massachusetts, when her husband was running for his second term as senator, she gave her first-ever campaign speech. She spoke to a French club—in French. She said it wasn't "as frightening as it would have been in English!" Compared to many of the wives of candidates, Jackie was younger and better dressed. Though he loved the way Jackie looked, Jack wasn't sure how the rest of the nation would react to his glamorous wife. "The American people just aren't ready for someone like you," he told her.

But was he wrong!

Everywhere she went during the presidential campaign, she attracted crowds. People came from near and far

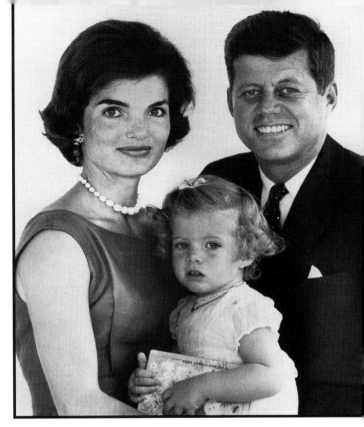

Jack and Jackie with their daughter, Caroline, in February 1960

to see the glamorous Jackie. She began to hold press conferences and fund-raising teas. She gave speeches in French, Italian, and Spanish when necessary. She organized listening parties for the debates between Jack and his opponent, Richard Nixon.

While Jackie still shied away from too much activity, she began to appreciate politics and what it could teach

Posters like the one shown here seemed to be everywhere during the campaign, and Jack Kennedy spoke at Democratic rallies all over the country, in cities large and small.

KENNEDY
FOR PRESIDENT

VOTE ⊗ **DEMOCRATIC**

her. It was the "most exciting life you can imagine," she said. You're "always involved with the news of the moment, meeting and working with people who are enormously alive, and every day you are caught up with something you really care about."

If she thought about what sort of First Lady she would be if Jack won

Opposite page: This New York City ticker-tape parade took place during the 1960 campaign.

the election, she never spoke about it. She was pregnant once again, and she was thinking a lot more about staying healthy. Jack did win the election that November. Three weeks later, Jackie gave birth to John Jr.

Now that the campaign was over, Jackie once again decided to make only those appearances that were necessary. "The official side of my life takes me away from my children a good deal," she said. "If I were to add

45

John F. Kennedy, Jr. (1960–)

☆ ☆

John F. Kennedy Jr.—John-John—was the first child ever to be born to a president-elect. This, and the fact that he was also born a Kennedy, seemed to destine him for politics. John, however, was much more interested in sports and acting throughout his school days. Nevertheless, when his uncle, Edward Kennedy, ran for president in 1988, John introduced him to the Democratic National Convention and the world television audience, winning a two-minute standing ovation from the crowd. After going to law school, John prosecuted criminals in New York City, always doing charity work in his spare time. In 1995, John blended the talents of both his parents by starting his political magazine *George*. He married Carolyn Bessette in 1996, thereby losing his title of America's most eligible bachelor.

political duties I would have practically no time with the children, and they're my first responsibility."

Jackie's family was very much on her mind as John F. Kennedy put his hand on the Bible and took his oath of office. Despite the bitter cold, the crowds cheered wildly. She, too, was very proud of her husband. "There was so much I wanted to say!" she remem-

Caroline Kennedy Schlossberg (1957–)

★ ★ ★ ★ ★ ★ ★ ★ ★ ★ ★ ★ ★ ★ ★ ★ ★ ★ ★ ★

Born on November 27, 1957, a day that Jacqueline Kennedy termed "the very happiest day of my life," Caroline Kennedy followed her mother's example—most of the time. The two did disagree about how Caroline dressed, and Caroline refused to be a debutante and make her formal entrance into society as her mother had done twenty-odd years before. Like her mother, she did spend time abroad, working in London for NBC. After college, she met and married Edwin Schlossberg, a designer of museums and educational exhibits and a fabulous cook. She went to law school and has written two books with her law-school friend Ellen Alderman—the most recent one dealing with the right to privacy. She writes in her home office so that she can be with her three children, Rose, Tatiana, and John. Following in her mother's footsteps, Caroline also works to support the arts and her father's legacy. She serves as president of the John F. Kennedy Library Foundation.

bered later. "But I could scarcely embrace him in front of all those people. So I remember I just put my hand on his cheek and said, 'Jack, you are so wonderful!' And he was smiling in the most touching and most vulnerable way. He looked so happy!"

Now, Jackie finally turned her thoughts to running the White House and setting a tone in the capital.

John Kennedy's inauguration speech was given on January 20, 1961, a freezing cold and snowy day in Washington, D.C.

Supreme Court Chief Justice Earl Warren administered the oath of office to John Fitzgerald Kennedy.

Raising her family out of the glare of television and newspapers would be Jackie's most difficult challenge. She wanted Caroline and John Jr. to grow up unspoiled and to lead as normal a life as possible. She complained that she felt as if she had "turned into a piece of public property," and did not want her children to experience that.

The Bergdorf Goodman Salon designed the cape and gown that Jacqueline Kennedy wore to the Inaugural Balls on January 20, 1961.

49

CHAPTER FIVE

First Lady

✫ ✫ ✫ ✫ ✫ ✫ ✫ ✫ ✫ ✫ ✫ ✫ ✫ ✫ ✫

Jacqueline Bouvier Kennedy was thirty-one years old when she became First Lady. She was the third youngest First Lady to live in the White House. Only Mrs. Grover Cleveland, who was twenty-one when she moved into the White House, and Mrs. John Tyler, who was twenty-four, were younger.

The role of American women, and First Ladies in particular, had changed by the time Julia Gardiner Tyler was First Lady in 1844 and Frances Folsom Cleveland was First Lady in 1886. Those roles had changed even further by the time Jackie Kennedy entered the White House in 1961.

✫ ✫ ✫ ✫ ✫ ✫ ✫ ✫ ✫ ✫ ✫ ✫ ✫ ✫ ✫

Julia Gardiner Tyler

Elizabeth "Bess" Wallace Truman

Frances Folsom Cleveland

Mamie Doud Eisenhower

Bess Truman and Mamie Eisenhower, the two First Ladies who lived in the White House immediately before Jackie, were very traditional. They acted as hostesses, took care of their families, and rarely ventured out in public. They were older women, grandmotherly, and much loved by the country. Jackie knew she could never be like them—nor did she want to be.

She was young and vivacious, with a growing family, many dogs and cats and rabbits, and interests that went beyond the traditional First Lady role. Like Eleanor Roosevelt, the First Lady who had lived in the White House before Mrs. Truman, Jackie would set new precedents as First Lady.

But what kind of First Lady would Jackie be? It was up to her to create an

Jack, Jackie, Caroline, John Jr., and several dogs enjoying the sunshine and fresh air while vacationing on Squaw Island off the coast of Cape Cod

Two-year-old John F. Kennedy Jr. having a good time rocking back and forth in his father's special rocking chair

Caroline, with her dolls, sits close to her mother in a window seat shortly after the Kennedys moved into the White House.

These four outfits were among dozens designed for Jacqueline Kennedy by Oleg Cassini during the first year Jackie spent as First Lady.

image. She knew people paid attention to what she wore but didn't want her clothes to become an issue for her husband. Because so many designers wanted to create clothes for her and newspapers wanted photos, she decided to hire an official designer who would be responsible for everything she wore. She also wanted to wear only American-made clothes, to showcase for the world fashions created here. She chose Oleg Cassini as her designer.

"I know that I am so much more of fashion interest than other First Ladies," she wrote to him. "I refuse to have Jack's administration plagued by fashion stories of a sensational manner." Cassini created what he called the "Jackie look," which included brightly colored clothes (Jackie loved pink, green, and yellow), simple dress-

Cassini designed this pink and white gown with Jackie's favorite colors in mind.

es, bouffant hairdos, and small square and round hats called pillboxes. Whether she wore casual clothes such as pink capri pants and an orange sweater or formal dresses such as a white silk ball gown with 20-button gloves, newspapers were hungry for the news.

In the first year alone, Cassini designed more than 100 outfits for the

Jackie wore this deep pink casual outfit during the 1962 Christmas holidays.

No Place Like Home

☆ ☆

Jacqueline Kennedy started the work that remade the White House into a national treasure, but to John and Caroline and all the other "first children" who had lived there, it was just home. John's favorite place to play was under his father's desk in the Oval Office. Caroline rode her pony, Macaroni, on the lawn. Archie Roosevelt, one of Theodore Roosevelt's four boys, loved to slide down the long staircase on a sterling silver tray that he got from the kitchen. Amy Carter enjoyed an addition to the White House grounds designed by her father, President Jimmy Carter—a treehouse!

First Lady. Jackie loved clothes, and she was particular about what she wore. She directed Cassini to make sure she was the only person to have any given dress. "Just make sure no one has exactly the same dress I do— the same color or material," she told him. "I want mine to be original, and no fat little women hopping around in the same dress." And yet, through it all, she found the public's interest in her clothes puzzling. "All the talk over what I wear and how I fix my hair has me amused," she said. "What does my hairdo have to do with my husband's ability to be president?"

But more than clothes mattered to Jackie. She was determined to create a "whole new atmosphere" in Washington. She wanted to turn it into the

Among the important pieces that Jackie Kennedy found during her search through the storage rooms and warehouses of the White House were the gold and silver flatware (left) made for President James Monroe and china (right) that had been used by President Abraham Lincoln.

A sofa that belonged to Dolley Madison now has a place of honor in the White House Red Room.

social and cultural center of the country, to bring great artists, musicians, actors, and intellectuals to the city, and to serve the best food and fine wine. And most of all, because of her love of art and architecture, she wanted to begin a movement to restore old buildings, not to knock them down.

The White House, with its 132 rooms, was a perfect starting point. Jackie had first visited the White House as an eleven-year-old child and long remembered how disappointed she was at the lack of history there, and that there was no book to take away recalling its rooms and history. When Jackie first moved in, she was disappointed again. What should be one of the grandest houses in the land was, in fact, one of the shabbiest. It was then that she became inspired to restore the White House. "I think the White House should show the wonderful heritage this country has," she said. "Presidents' wives have an obligation to contribute something. . . . People who visit the White House see practically nothing that dates before 1900. Young people should see things that develop their sense of history."

Jackie began her journey to restore the White House by ordering from the Library of Congress every book or article about the mansion's history. She pored over more than 40 such books. "Everything in the White House must have a reason for being there," she said. "It would be a sacrilege merely to redecorate—a word I hate. It must be *restored* and that has nothing to do with decoration. This is a question of scholarship."

Within a month of moving into the White House, Jackie formed the Fine Arts Committee for the White House. The committee raised money, asked for donations of antiques, and bought antique furniture that past presidents had used. Jackie rummaged through the storage rooms and warehouses of the White House, too, in her search. Eventually, she found many important objects.

She found George Washington's armchair, gold and silver flatware made around 1817 in France for President James Monroe, a sofa belonging to Dolley Madison, china that had been used by President Abraham Lincoln in the 1860s, and rugs woven for President Theodore Roosevelt in 1902, as well as dishes, paintings, and other furniture.

Her work on the White House became so popular that when she gave a guided tour of the mansion on television so that the people of the United States could see all she had done, 56 million people watched. A guidebook written about the mansion sold more than 600,000 copies in its first year.

"The White House is as it should be," she said finally. "It's all I ever dreamed for it."

Jackie gave a televised guided tour of the White House after her restoration project was completed

Cellist Pablo Casals was one of the many fine musicians Jackie invited to perform at the White House.

Jackie was able to live out other dreams while First Lady, as well. Now that the White House was a glittering success, she began to invite some of the world's finest musicians and actors to perform there. The great cellist Pablo Casals, violinist Isaac Stern, and actor Basil Rathbone all performed at the Kennedy White House. She entertained lavishly, even once throwing a gala for the president of Pakistan at Mount Vernon, George Washington's home in Virginia. All 140 guests sailed up the Potomac River from the capital to Mount

Jacqueline Kennedy entertained the president of Pakistan at a Mount Vernon gala.

The Kennedys hosted a brilliant party in honor of every living Nobel Prize winner.

Musicians, statesmen, and Nobel Prize winners were not the only honored guests at the Kennedy White House. This group gathered in the East Room to hear famous actor Fredric March give a reading.

Noble Nobel

✮ ✮

Alfred Nobel was called the "Dynamite King." A Swedish inventor and chemist who lived in the last century, Nobel found a way to use the explosive nitroglycerin more safely by forming it into sticks. Strongly opposed to the military uses of his invention, called dynamite, he left money to fund the Nobel Prizes. Achievers in the areas of physics, chemistry, medicine, literature, and peace receive what is now considered the highest honor in the world. As a promoter of peace, Alfred Nobel would be pleased to know that today more people associate him with the Peace Prize than with an explosive.

Vernon, where they dined under the stars and danced the night away to the music of the National Symphony. One party she hosted was in honor of every living Nobel Prize winner. "I think this is the most extraordinary collection of talent, of human knowledge, that has ever been gathered together at the White House," said the president that night, "with the possible exception of when Thomas Jefferson dined alone."

Jackie helped raise funds for the National Cultural Center (now the Kennedy Center for the Performing Arts) and supported the arts in any way she was asked. In fact, she arranged for the loan of the famous *Mona Lisa* painting from the French government and had it displayed at the National Gallery of Art. Thousands of schoolchildren were brought to see it.

Though Jackie worked to bring history and elegance back to the capital—and to the United States—there was still an entire world to conquer. And conquer she did. Just as she won praise at home for her tireless work on behalf of the arts, she also was admired throughout the world.

In 1961, Jackie accompanied the president to Europe on her first official

As First Lady, Jackie helped raise funds for the National Cultural Center (above and right) in Washington, D.C. Later named the Kennedy Center for the Performing Arts in honor of John F. Kennedy, the grand opening featured a work called Mass, which was composed for the occasion by Leonard Bernstein (below, right).

visit as First Lady. Landing at the airport in Paris, the couple was greeted by thousands of cheering people. More than 200,000 people lined the roads through the city shouting, *"Vive Jackie! Vive Jackie!"* ("Long live Jackie! Long live Jackie!"). She was written about and photographed so often in France that at one gathering President Kennedy introduced himself by saying, "I am the man who accompanied Jacqueline Kennedy to Paris!"

In Vienna, she stopped traffic.

In England, people lined the streets as well. Queen Elizabeth and Prince Philip hosted a dinner at Buckingham Palace for the presidential couple. The trip to Europe was a total success and secured Jackie's place as one of the most influential persons in the world. The *Boston Globe* went as far as to report that Europe loved the First Lady so much that while there she had shaken 8,042 hands and had her own hand kissed 867 times!

The following year, she went to India with her sister. There, she visited the Taj Mahal, rode elephants, watched snake charmers, and was entertained by maharajahs. People

Jackie with French President Charles DeGaulle during the Kennedys' 1961 trip to France

During their European trip, the Kennedys were entertained at Buckingham Palace by Queen Elizabeth (second from right) and Prince Philip (left).

On Jackie's 1962 trip to India, she was greeted by huge crowds of cheering people (above). One highlight of the trip was an elephant ride she took with her sister, Lee (right).

shouted *"Amriki Rani, Amriki Rani"* ("American Queen! American Queen!"). In Pakistan, 100,000 people waited to greet her. That country's president gave her a thoroughbred stallion, which eventually became her favorite horse. But Jackie traveled far beyond Europe during her years as First Lady. She also visited Mexico, Venezuela, Canada, Greece, Colombia, Turkey, and Morocco.

Jackie's life had changed in many ways as First Lady, though she still was not fond of making political appearances. When it became known that she was pregnant again with her third

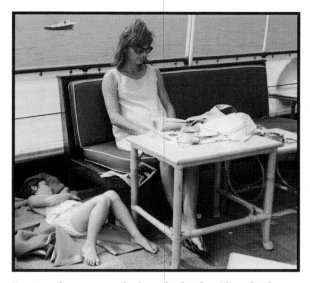

During the summer before the birth of her third child, Jackie relaxed off the coast of Cape Cod and took care of her health.

child in 1963, she told her secretary to clear her schedule. She planned on doing little but taking care of her health while awaiting the birth of the baby in August. In fact, from the time she announced she was pregnant to

the time she gave birth she appeared in public only twice—once at a dinner in honor of the Duchess of Luxembourg and once in New York for a performance by England's Royal Ballet. She spent the rest of the spring and summer at an isolated house on Squaw Island, off the coast of Cape Cod.

All the waiting for the baby would end in tragedy. Weeks before the baby was due, she was rushed to the hospital. She gave birth to a boy, who was named Patrick. Other than the fact that he came earlier than expected, it had seemed like a normal birth. But Patrick was born with an infection and died less than two days later.

Months went by in which she mourned her loss. In November, when the president suggested she might like to accompany him on the campaign swing through Texas, she accepted.

☆ ☆ ☆ ☆ ☆ ☆ ☆ ☆ ☆ ☆ ☆ ☆ ☆ ☆ ☆

CHAPTER SIX

The Last Days in Washington

☆ ☆ ☆ ☆ ☆ ☆ ☆ ☆ ☆ ☆ ☆ ☆ ☆ ☆ ☆

When Jackie returned to the White House, still stunned after her husband's assassination, she sprang into action. She ordered her aides to collect everything written about the funeral of another great president who had changed the world and had been assassinated as well, almost exactly 100 years before: President Abraham Lincoln. She had her assistants study those books and pictures and used Lincoln's funeral as a model for her husband's.

For two days, the president's body lay in the Capitol Rotunda, the coffin draped with an American flag. More than 250,000 people passed by, many weeping,

☆ ☆ ☆ ☆ ☆ ☆ ☆ ☆ ☆ ☆ ☆ ☆ ☆ ☆ ☆

Saying Good-bye to Another President

When President Abraham Lincoln was assassinated in 1865, the nation expressed its shock and grief with sixteen days of funeral processions and memorial services. After days of ceremony in Washington, D.C., President Lincoln's body was carried on a special train across the country to Springfield, Illinois, to be buried. In the twelve cities where the train stopped, thousands of Americans silently stood in line for hours to pay their respects. Along the route, both day and night, people crowded the tracks just to get a glimpse as the train moved past.

President Kennedy's body lay in a flag-draped coffin in the Capitol Rotunda for three days.

Jackie and Caroline saying good-bye to the president on the day before the funeral

John F. Kennedy Jr., on his third birthday, salutes his father's coffin as it is carried from St. Matthew's Cathedral after the funeral.

many staring in disbelief. Jackie took Caroline there on the day before the funeral. "We're going to say good-bye to Daddy," she whispered to Caroline, "and we're going to kiss him good-bye and tell Daddy how much we love him and how much we'll always miss him." Caroline knelt and hesitated for a second. Jackie said, "You know, you just

Jackie walked behind her husband's horse-drawn caisson from the Capitol to St. Matthew's Cathedral for the funeral. She was flanked by the president's brothers and followed by dozens of world leaders.

kiss." With that, the little girl bent down and kissed the flag that draped the coffin.

On the day of the funeral, Jackie, dressed in black, walked slowly behind the horse-drawn caisson that held her husband's coffin. The procession moved slowly from the Capitol toward St. Matthew's Cathedral, the church at which the Kennedys had worshipped, for the funeral. More than a million people lined the street watching in silence. Jackie, walking between the president's two brothers, was followed by dozens of world leaders—including presidents, prime ministers, kings, and queens—all of whom had come to pay their respects.

The streets along the way were lined with people as President Kennedy's funeral procession moved slowly from St. Matthew's Cathedral to Arlington National Cemetery, where the president was to be buried.

After the service, the caisson bore the president's casket along Connecticut Avenue, past the Lincoln Memorial, on its way to Arlington National Cemetery. On a hill at Arlington, where the president was to be buried, 50 fighter jets flew in formation in honor of their fallen leader. Mrs. Kennedy lit the eternal flame, which would burn forever in the president's memory. There was a 21-gun salute. Then, as the afternoon air began to chill, taps was played on a lone bugle, the American flag that had draped the coffin was neatly folded and given to the widowed First Lady, and the president's body was lowered into the ground.

A National Resting Place

★ ★

John F. Kennedy shares his final resting place at Arlington National Cemetery with more than 200,000 other souls. Occupying 612 acres (248 hectares) of rolling hillside overlooking the Potomac River just outside of Washington, D.C., this vast national shrine was established as a Civil War burial ground. Today, American soldiers from every war since the Revolution rest at Arlington, along with thousands of other military personnel. Heavyweight boxer Joe Louis and detective novelist Dashiell Hammett, both soldiers during World War II, are buried here, as are America's youngest soldier and the first woman army surgeon. Two presidents, John F. Kennedy and William Howard Taft, rest at Arlington. The Tomb of the Unknowns contains the remains of one unidentified soldier from World War I, World War II, the Korean War, and the Vietnam War. These four soldiers, forever nameless, silently represent all of America's war dead.

After Kennedy's burial service at Arlington National Cemetery, the American flag that had draped his coffin was folded and given to his widow.

There was still one more, very important thing to be done. After all, this was November 25, and though she had just attended her husband's funeral, it was also John Jr.'s third birthday. Though some family members thought there should be no party on this solemn day, Jackie insisted there be a small celebration in the White House family quarters. John Jr. might be too young to understand the death and funeral of his father, she thought, but he wasn't too young to be disappointed by not having a birthday party. So candles were lit, cake was served, and he opened his presents with his mother at his side.

This day, starting with a funeral and ending with a birthday, held every emotion for Jackie. The country had seen the grace, style, courage, and spirit by which she lived. It was because of her serenity and dignity during this awful time, many later said, that the people of the country were able to stand tall, share their grief, and console one another.

While her husband's assassination was the end of her role as First Lady, it was also to mark the beginning of her new role as an independent woman. To the White House she had brought her elegance, love of the arts, and her belief that though she was married to the president of the United States, she was still a person, a wife, and a mother.

"If you bungle raising your children," she once said, "I don't think whatever else you do well matters very much."

Upon leaving the White House and until the day she died, Jacqueline Kennedy continued to live by the same ideals she had lived by until that night when her husband's three-year-old namesake blew out the candles on his cake.

After the assassination, it took less than two weeks for Jackie to pack the family's belongings and move out of the White House. The new president's wife, Lady Bird Johnson, had invited Jackie to stay as long as she needed to. But Jackie was in a hurry.

The White House held too many memories. Every time she turned a corner, Jackie thought of Jack. She kept only one photo of him nearby. And it was one of him taken from behind, nine days before he died. "It

After leaving the White House, which had been their home for nearly three years, Jackie and her children moved into this house in Washington, D.C.

was the only picture I could have around for months," she said. "I just couldn't look at his face."

There was one more thing she had to do before leaving the White House for good, however. She had a plaque made for the mantel of their bedroom. It said: "In this room lived John Fitzgerald Kennedy with his wife Jacqueline during the two years, ten months, and two days he was president of the United States."

Jackie moved into a house in Washington and began to face the mountain of mail she had received during the past few weeks. She would never be able to answer it all she thought. There was only one thing to

John F. Kennedy's brothers, Edward (left) and Robert, accompanied Jacqueline as she appeared on television to thank the viewers for their messages and tributes after her husband's death.

do. She would have to go on television to thank the viewers for their kindness.

"I want to take this opportunity to express my appreciation for the hundreds and thousands of messages— nearly 800,000 in all—which my children and I have received over the past few weeks," she told millions of viewers. "The knowledge of the affection in which my husband was held by all of you has sustained me, and the warmth of these tributes is something I shall never forget."

★ ★ ★ ★ ★ ★ ★ ★ ★ ★ ★ ★ ★ ★ ★

CHAPTER SEVEN

Jackie O

* * * * * * * * * * * * * * * *

Jackie, still one of the most famous and admired women in the world, craved privacy. But all day long, crowds of people would stand in front of her Washington house, hoping to catch a glimpse of her or the children. She felt like a fish in a fishbowl. Jackie soon packed up the house and family and headed to New York, where she thought they could live in peace.

Though she was urged to run for the Senate, or to write a newspaper column, or even to become the U.S. ambassador to France, she said no to all suggestions. Her time now was devoted to raising her children and creating memorials to her slain husband. She was, it

* * * * * * * * * * * * * * * *

Jackie, John, and Caroline spent the 1963 Christmas holidays in Aspen, Colorado.

Cape Canaveral, site of the John F. Kennedy Space Center (left), was renamed Cape Kennedy in honor of President Kennedy. The original name was restored to the cape in 1973, though the space center itself retains the Kennedy name.

Jackie helped raise funds for the John Fitzgerald Kennedy Library at the University of Massachusetts.

turns out, very good at doing both. First, she persuaded President Johnson to rename Cape Canaveral, site of the Florida space center, Cape Kennedy. (Its original name was restored in 1973.) She began to raise funds for what would eventually become the John F. Kennedy Library at the University of Massachusetts, just outside Boston.

81

All in the Family

John Kennedy and his two brothers all wanted to be president. Three presidential candidates in one family is pretty extraordinary. To John (Jack) Kennedy and his brothers Robert (Bobby) and Edward (Ted), however, politics was the family business. Both of the boys' grandfathers had been Boston politicians. Their father, a very powerful man in politics and business, had also served as ambassador to Great Britain. The three Kennedy brothers inherited a lot of power and many important connections. However, just as in a family-owned business, the name alone doesn't draw people—or votes. The Kennedys brought talent, a sense of duty, and a philosophy of hard work to their bids for the presidency. Sadly, an asssassin's bullet killed Bobby in the middle of his campaign in 1968. Although Ted has never won the presidency, he has served many long and dedicated years in the U.S. Senate.

Jackie returned to the political scene briefly when Robert F. Kennedy, her husband's brother, ran for president in 1968. She was very close to him. Then tragedy struck again. In Los Angeles for a campaign speech, he, too, was shot down. His death once again rocked Jackie's world. She became ever more concerned for her family's safety.

"I hate this country," she said angrily after this second assassination. "If they're killing Kennedys, my children are number one targets. I want to get out of this country."

Jackie, whose every move was chronicled in the press, made a shocking announcement later that year. She planned to marry Greek shipping tycoon Aristotle (Ari) Onassis in October 1968. She was thirty-nine years old. He was sixty-two. "Jackie, how could you?" read one newspaper headline. Much of the press, and the Kennedy family, were against the marriage. But Jackie was firm. When one

CHICAGO SUN-TIMES

★ ★ ★ ★
F I N A L
TURF EDITION

WEATHER
Sunny and hot Thursday. Chance of rain. High near 90. See Page 128.

© 1968 by Field Enterprises Inc.

Vol. 21, No. 108   Phone 321-3000   THURSDAY, JUNE 6, 1968   152 Pages—10 Cents

RFK DEAD!

Assassin Bullet Kills Senator

By David Murray
Sun-Times Correspondent

LOS ANGELES—Sen. Robert F. Kennedy died early Thursday morning in Good Samaritan Hospital here.

Death came to the New York senator about 25 hours after he was struck by shots from an assassin's pistol.

Moments before he was shot, Sen. Kennedy had spoken to a crowd of supporters who had gathered in the Ambassador Hotel to cheer his victory in the California primary.

The announcement of his death was made to about 100 reporters gathered in the makeshift pressroom at Good Samaritan Hospital.

Frank Mankiewicz, the New York senator's press secretary, was grim-faced and with the strain of the last 25 hours showing deeply in his face, as he told the newsmen Sen. Kennedy had died.

Outside, across the street from the hospital, the crowd heard the news quietly for the most part, but a few began openly weeping.

One Negro man, walking up the hill to the hospital, was racked by great, groaning sobs.

Inside the pressroom, reporters, many of them admirers of Sen. Kennedy, went about their sad tasks with their eyes misted over with tears. After they relayed the announcement to their offices around the country, they waited for former White House press secretary Pierre Salinger to arrive and discuss funeral plans for the 42-year old Democrat.

In eight short years Sen. Kennedy had blazed a political trail across the country which could never be forgotten. He died at the height of his 1968 campaign for the Presidency.

With the senator when he died were his wife Ethel, his sisters Mrs. Stephen Smith and Mrs. Patricia Smith, his brother-in-law Stephen Smith and his sister-in-law Mrs. John F. Kennedy.

Early, Wednesday surgeons had removed from his brain all but a fragment of a bullet police said was fired by a young gunman of Jordanian heritage.

At 7:33 p.m. Chicago time, Mankiewicz, his face deeply etched with strain and fatigue, mounted the lectern in the

Turn to Page 4

LBJ Mourns 'Tragic Loss'

WASHINGTON (AP)—President Johnson issued this statement on learning of the death of Sen. Robert F. Kennedy:

This is a time of tragedy and loss. Sen. Robert F. Kennedy is dead. Robert Kennedy affirmed this country—affirmed the essential decency of its people, their longing for peace, their desire to improve conditions of life for all.

During his life, he knew far more than his share of personal tragedy.

Yet he never abandoned his faith in America. He never lost his confidence in the spiritual strength of ordinary men and women.

He believed in the capacity of the young for excellence and in the right of the old and poor to a life of dignity. Our public life is diminished by his loss.

Mrs. Johnson and I extend our deepest sympathy to Mrs. Kennedy and his family.

I have issued a proclamation calling upon our nation to observe a day of mourning for Robert Kennedy.

**ROBERT FRANCIS KENNEDY
(1925-1968)**

People who went to bed early on the night of June 5, l968, awoke to shocking headlines like the one that appeared in the Chicago Sun–Times.

---

friend told her she'd fall off her pedestal by marrying Onassis, her response said it all. "It's better than freezing up there," she said.

Onassis and Jackie had a stormy marriage. Though they had everything a person could possibly want—lavish homes, a yacht, and even a private island in the Mediterranean Sea— they were missing one thing. Com-

83

This picture of Aristotle Onassis, Jacqueline Kennedy Onassis, and Jackie's daughter, Caroline Kennedy, was taken just after the Onassis wedding ceremony.

panionship. Both were independent souls. They enjoyed each other's company but had different interests. He liked to smoke cigars and make business deals. She liked to travel, shop for clothes, and attend the theater. They were rarely home at the same time. In fact, they were rarely even in the same country! As the

years passed, they grew apart, and he even contemplated divorce.

Onassis, though, was not well. In March 1975, after six-and-a-half years of marriage, he died. "Aristotle Onassis rescued me at a moment when my life was engulfed with shadows," Jackie said after his death. "He meant a lot to me. He brought me into a

The Onassis yacht, Christina, was named for the daughter of Aristotle Onassis.

Jackie bicycling in Central Park with her son, John

Jackie and the designer look at proofs of a book she edited for Viking Press.

world where one could find both happiness and love. We lived through many beautiful experiences together which cannot be forgotten, and for which I will be eternally grateful."

Jackie O, as she had been referred to since her marriage to Onassis, was now independent. She was also now very, very wealthy. Though she still wished to remain as private a person as possible, she returned to live full-time in her apartment in New York. She was, for the first time, free to do and be anything she wanted.

In 1975, Jackie took a job—her first since her days at the *Washington Times–Herald*. A friend had suggested that her love of art and literature would enable her to be a good book editor. She agreed. When an offer came her way, she accepted it. Within a few years, she was very successful. When her company planned to publish a fictional story about the assassination of another of John F. Kennedy's brothers, however, she quit in protest.

Another company hired her, though, and she worked there until the end of her life. "I'm drawn to books that are out of our regular expe-

Worth a Thousand Words

★ ★

After her nearly 60 years in the public eye, it is hard to say which is the most familiar image of the legendary Jacqueline Bouvier Kennedy Onassis. In early por-

traits, she gazes serenely into the camera's lens, as yet untroubled by life's difficulties. Many Americans remember her best as the glamorous First Lady. Pictures show her dark hair coiffed into a trend-setting bouffant or brushed smoothly into place under her famous pillbox hat. The camera record-ed her over and over again on the arm of a dashing JFK, ele-gantly attired for an important evening or event. Indelibly etched in many American minds are the famous images of the distressed widow in her bright pink suit on the day the president was assassinated, or standing sadly at the gravesite with her two young children. A younger generation remembers "Jackie O," who was a favorite with the paparazzi, or tabloid photographers. As if to escape their prying cameras, she covered her head with scarves and hid her familiar face behind oversized sunglasses. No matter how she is remembered, however, she will always be Jackie.

Jackie's crusade against the demolition of New York City's St. Bartholomew's Church was successful. The church, surrounded by skyscrapers, still stands.

rience, books of other cultures, of ancient histories," she said. "To me, a wonderful book is one that takes me on a journey into something I didn't know before." She edited books on Russian art and history, children's books, fairy tales, and even Michael Jackson's autobiography.

In addition to her professional activities, Jackie occasionally took part in civic life. Because of her lifelong passion for architecture and historic preservation, she became involved in saving old buildings in New York. It was a rare instance of her taking a public stand.

When St. Bartholomew's Church wanted to demolish its buildings and erect a 59-story skyscraper, she protested. "The future of New York City is

Jackie appeared at a news conference to try to sway public opinion against building an office tower at the southwest corner of Central Park on the site of the New York Coliseum.

Jackie smiles broadly in Boston on May 29, 1990, at the dedication of a John F. Kennedy statue.

bleak if landmark laws no longer apply to religious institutions," she told the state senate. "I think that if you cut people off from what nourishes them spiritually or historically then something inside them dies." She won that battle, as well as one involving the New York Coliseum, on the southwest

Jacqueline Kennedy Onassis lived full-time in this New York City Fifth Avenue apartment building during the last nineteen years of her life.

Going. . .Going. . .Gone!

✫ ✫

Golf clubs, diamonds, desks, baskets, and magazines: imagine having your personal possessions sell for $34.5 million! That's what happened when the belongings of Jacqueline Kennedy Onassis were auctioned off after her death. True to her final wishes, Jackie's children, John and Caroline, gave many important documents and photographs—along with their mother's wedding dress—to the Kennedy Library. The rest they put up for sale. The auction caused much excitement for four days in April 1996. Everybody, it seemed, wanted to own a remembrance of the stunning woman who had set so many American styles and touched so many lives. Few, however, could afford the prices. The 40-carat diamond engagement ring given to her by Aristotle Onassis drew the largest bid at $2.5 million. Even a collection of ordinary baskets sold for nearly $10,000 and a silver tape measure for four times that. Items belonging to JFK were popular as well, including golf clubs (bought by Arnold Schwarzenegger), a humidor (to hold cigars), and the desk at which the president signed the treaty to ban nuclear testing in 1963. The proceeds of the sale will be saved for Jackie's grandchildren.

corner of Central Park. A real-estate magnate wanted to rip it down and build a huge office tower. Once again, Jackie sprang into action. The new building, she said, would create a mile-long shadow over the park. "It's a monstrous idea," she said at a rally. "It's our responsibility to voice concern when we feel the city's future is in danger."

Though she was one of the most celebrated women alive, over the years, New York did provide the peace for which she had been searching. Her children were able to attend private schools there. They both eventually became lawyers. Jackie was able to go to work and out to dinner and, while always recognized, was rarely bothered. She exercised regularly by walking in Central Park with her children and, in later years, with her grandchildren, Rose, Tatiana, and John.

John F. Kennedy Jr. leaves his mother's apartment building early on the day Jackie died. Jackie's family and closest friends spent the difficult days at her side.

In 1994, Jackie became ill. She checked into the hospital and was told she had cancer. It had spread throughout her body and there was little the doctors could do. She said that she wanted to go home to die.

That May, in front of Jackie's Fifth Avenue apartment building, crowds gathered, some sobbing openly, others holding roses or candles. Police blocked off the area in front so that Jackie's family and friends could enter

Caroline Kennedy leaves her mother's home the morning after Jackie's death. While family and friends had kept vigil inside the apartment, crowds of mourners—and photographers—kept vigil outside.

and pay their last respects. Caroline and John stayed by her side.

On May 19, Jackie died peacefully in her own bed in her own home.

"Last night, at around ten-fifteen, my mother passed on," John Kennedy said, standing in front of his mother's building. "She was surrounded by her friends and her family and her books and the people and things she loved . . . and now she's in God's hands."

Jackie was sixty-four when she

Portrait of America, 1994: Earthshaking Events

✮ ✮

The new year of 1994 was only weeks old when a violent earthquake rattled Los Angeles, California, at dawn on January 18. At 6.6 on the Richter scale, the quake was the strongest to hit the city in this century. Thirty-four people died, highways crumbled, and houses burned. For Angelenos, it was a frightening way to start the year, and it set the tone for twelve months of earthshaking events.

In June, Los Angeles was rocked again by news of the brutal murder of football star O. J. Simpson's former wife, Nicole, and her friend, Ron Goldman. For the rest of the year, Americans closely followed the events surrounding the investigation and trial. Prime suspect Simpson would be found not guilty of the murders the following year. In November, across the country in Washington, President Bill Clinton received a shocking message from voters. Americans were unhappy with the way he and his party, the Democrats, were running the country. For the first time in 40 years, Republicans won a majority in both the House of Representatives and the Senate. To get laws made and bills passed, the president and the Congress would have to find new ways to work together. Several former presidents made the news as well. Richard Nixon died at the age of eighty-one, and Ronald Reagan revealed that he was battling Alzheimer's disease. Jimmy Carter

died. She had been a society deb, a newspaper reporter, the First Lady, a book editor, a wife, and a mother. Throughout her life, though lived in the public eye, she fought to maintain her dignity and individuality.

"People often forget that I was Jacqueline Bouvier before being Mrs. Kennedy or Mrs. Onassis," she once wrote to a reporter. "Throughout my life I have always tried to remain true to myself. . . . Every moment one lives is different from the other, the good, the bad, the hardship, the joy, the helped make strides toward peace in Bosnia by negotiating a cease-fire there between Serbs and Croats.

Science rocked, too, especially in space. A Dutch-American-British team discovered a new galaxy, called Dwingeloo 1, located behind the constellation of Cassiopeia. And astronomers were thrilled when they were able to watch twenty-one pieces of a huge comet crash into Jupiter and explode into fireballs. Back on Earth, scientists unearthed the first fossilized embryo of a meat-eating dinosaur.

The world of sports reeled as a major-league baseball strike canceled the World Series for the first time since 1904. Controversy shook the Winter Olympics held in Norway, especially among the American figure skaters. When Nancy Kerrigan was attacked a month before the games by a man with a crowbar, everyone blamed her rival Tonya Harding. At the games, Kerrigan skated away with a silver medal, while Harding was unable to place. In happier Olympic news, the United States won its Winter Games record of 13 medals. Speed skater Bonnie Blair brought her career total to 5 medals, a record for any American woman in the Olympic Games.

Americans escaped this earthshaking year at movies such as *The Lion King* and *Pulp Fiction*. Surprisingly, a quiet movie about a gentle man named Forrest Gump won the Academy Award for best picture.

tragedy. Love and happiness are all interwoven into one single indescribable whole that is called life."

Jacqueline Bouvier Kennedy Onassis had been a symbol in America for much of what was good and dignified. When she died, many felt, an era of grace and spirit died along with her.

☆ ☆ ☆ ☆ ☆ ☆ ☆ ☆ ☆ ☆ ☆ ☆ ☆ ☆ ☆ ☆

The Presidents and Their First Ladies

President YEARS IN OFFICE	Birth–Death	First Lady	Birth–Death
1789–1797 George Washington	1732–1799	Martha Dandridge Custis Washington	1731–1802
1797–1801 John Adams	1735–1826	Abigail Smith Adams	1744–1818
1801–1809 Thomas Jefferson†	1743–1826		
1809–1817 James Madison	1751–1836	Dolley Payne Todd Madison	1768–1849
1817–1825 James Monroe	1758–1831	Elizabeth Kortright Monroe	1768–1830
1825–1829 John Quincy Adams	1767–1848	Louisa Catherine Johnson Adams	1775–1852
1829–1837 Andrew Jackson†	1767–1845		
1837–1841 Martin Van Buren†	1782–1862		
1841 William Henry Harrison‡	1773–1841		
1841–1845 John Tyler	1790–1862	Letitia Christian Tyler (1841–1842) Julia Gardiner Tyler (1844–1845)	1790–1842 1820–1889
1845–1849 James K. Polk	1795–1849	Sarah Childress Polk	1803–1891
1849–1850 Zachary Taylor	1784–1850	Margaret Mackall Smith Taylor	1788–1852
1850–1853 Millard Fillmore	1800–1874	Abigail Powers Fillmore	1798–1853
1853–1857 Franklin Pierce	1804–1869	Jane Means Appleton Pierce	1806–1863
1857–1861 James Buchanan*	1791–1868		
1861–1865 Abraham Lincoln	1809–1865	Mary Todd Lincoln	1818–1882
1865–1869 Andrew Johnson	1808–1875	Eliza McCardle Johnson	1810–1876
1869–1877 Ulysses S. Grant	1822–1885	Julia Dent Grant	1826–1902
1877–1881 Rutherford B. Hayes	1822–1893	Lucy Ware Webb Hayes	1831–1889
1881 James A. Garfield	1831–1881	Lucretia Rudolph Garfield	1832–1918
1881–1885 Chester A. Arthur†	1829–1886		

† wife died before he took office ‡ wife too ill to accompany him to Washington * never married

1885–1889			
Grover Cleveland	1837–1908	Frances Folsom Cleveland	1864–1947
1889–1893			
Benjamin Harrison	1833–1901	Caroline Lavinia Scott Harrison	1832–1892
1893–1897			
Grover Cleveland	1837–1908	Frances Folsom Cleveland	1864–1947
1897–1901			
William McKinley	1843–1901	Ida Saxton McKinley	1847–1907
1901–1909			
Theodore Roosevelt	1858–1919	Edith Kermit Carow Roosevelt	1861–1948
1909–1913			
William Howard Taft	1857–1930	Helen Herron Taft	1861–1943
1913–1921			
Woodrow Wilson	1856–1924	Ellen Louise Axson Wilson (1913–1914)	1860–1914
		Edith Bolling Galt Wilson (1915–1921)	1872–1961
1921–1923			
Warren G. Harding	1865–1923	Florence Kling Harding	1860–1924
1923–1929			
Calvin Coolidge	1872–1933	Grace Anna Goodhue Coolidge	1879–1957
1929–1933			
Herbert Hoover	1874–1964	Lou Henry Hoover	1874–1944
1933–1945			
Franklin D. Roosevelt	1882–1945	Anna Eleanor Roosevelt	1884–1962
1945–1953			
Harry S. Truman	1884–1972	Bess Wallace Truman	1885–1982
1953–1961			
Dwight D. Eisenhower	1890–1969	Mamie Geneva Doud Eisenhower	1896–1979
1961–1963			
John F. Kennedy	1917–1963	Jacqueline Bouvier Kennedy	1929–1994
1963–1969			
Lyndon B. Johnson	1908–1973	Claudia Taylor (Lady Bird) Johnson	1912–
1969–1974			
Richard Nixon	1913–1994	Patricia Ryan Nixon	1912–1993
1974–1977			
Gerald Ford	1913–	Elizabeth Bloomer Ford	1918–
1977–1981			
James Carter	1924–	Rosalynn Smith Carter	1927–
1981–1989			
Ronald Reagan	1911–	Nancy Davis Reagan	1923–
1989–1993			
George Bush	1924–	Barbara Pierce Bush	1925–
1993–			
William Jefferson Clinton	1946–	Hillary Rodham Clinton	1947–

Jacqueline Bouvier
Kennedy Onassis Timeline

1929	✭	St. Valentine's Day Massacre takes place in Chicago
		Jacqueline Bouvier is born on July 28
		Stock market crashes and the Great Depression begins
1931	✭	"The Star-Spangled Banner" becomes the national anthem
		Empire State Building is opened in New York City
1932	✭	Franklin D. Roosevelt is elected president
		Amelia Earhart becomes the first woman to fly solo across the Atlantic Ocean
1933	✭	President Roosevelt begins the New Deal to end the Great Depression
1934	✭	Nylon is invented
1935	✭	Congress passes the Social Security Act
1936	✭	Franklin D. Roosevelt is reelected president
1937	✭	*Hindenburg* crashes in New Jersey
		Golden Gate Bridge in San Francisco is dedicated
1938	✭	Jacqueline Bouvier's parents are divorced
1939	✭	World War II begins
1940	✭	Franklin D. Roosevelt is reelected president
		Average U.S. life expectancy is 64 years
1941	✭	Japan bombs Pearl Harbor and the United States enters World War II
1942	✭	Japanese forces capture the Philippines
1943	✭	John F. Kennedy is given command of PT-109 in the South Pacific
1944	✭	Franklin D. Roosevelt is reelected president
		Rome, Paris, and the Philippines are liberated

1945	★	Franklin D. Roosevelt dies
		Harry S. Truman becomes president
		Germany and Japan surrender, ending World War II
1946	★	John F. Kennedy is elected to the U.S. House of Representatives
1947	★	Jackie Robinson becomes the first African American to play major-league baseball
1948	★	John F. Kennedy is reelected to the U.S. House of Representatives
		Harry S. Truman is elected president
1949	★	United Nations Headquarters is dedicated in New York City
1950	★	United States enters Korean War
		John F. Kennedy is reelected to the U.S. House of Representatives
1952	★	Jacqueline Bouvier becomes a reporter for the *Washington Times–Herald*
		Dwight D. Eisenhower is elected president
		John F. Kennedy is elected to the U.S. Senate
1953	★	Korean War ends
		Jacqueline Bouvier marries John F. Kennedy
1954	★	Supreme Court declares segregated schools to be unconstitutional
		Ernest Hemingway wins the Nobel Prize in literature
1956	★	Dwight D. Eisenhower is reelected president
1957	★	Scientists link cigarette smoking and lung cancer
		Caroline Bouvier Kennedy is born
1958	★	John F. Kennedy is reelected to the U.S. Senate
1959	★	Alaska and Hawaii become states
1960	★	John F. Kennedy and Richard M. Nixon take part in the first televised debates between presidential candidates
		John F. Kennedy is elected president
		John F. Kennedy Jr. is born

1961	★	Bay of Pigs invasion fails
		Berlin Wall separates East and West Berlin
		First Americans fly in space
		Peace Corps is established
		United States sends aid and troops to South Vietnam
1962	★	Jacqueline Kennedy takes the nation on a televised tour of the restored White House
		Cuban missile crisis forces the Soviet Union to dismantle missiles in Cuba
1963	★	March on Washington is held for civil rights
		Patrick Bouvier Kennedy is born and dies two days later
		John F. Kennedy is assassinated
		Lyndon B. Johnson becomes president
1964	★	Lyndon B. Johnson is elected president
		Civil Rights Act of 1964 is passed
1965	★	Malcolm X is assassinated
		Riots break out in Los Angeles' Watts neighborhood
1966	★	Congress passes the Medicare Act
1968	★	Martin Luther King Jr. and Robert F. Kennedy are assassinated
		Jacqueline Kennedy marries Aristotle Onassis
		Richard M. Nixon is elected president
1969	★	President Nixon withdraws 110,000 soldiers from Vietnam
		U.S. astronauts land on the moon
1970	★	Antiwar protests rock college campuses
1972	★	Last U.S. ground troops are withdrawn from Vietnam
		Richard Nixon is reelected president
1973	★	Burglary at Democratic headquarters in the Watergate complex is reported
1974	★	Richard M. Nixon resigns from office because of the Watergate scandal
		Gerald Ford becomes president
		President Ford grants Nixon a pardon

1975	★	Aristotle Onassis dies
		South Vietnam falls to the Communists
		Jacqueline Onassis becomes an editor at Viking
1976	★	Jimmy Carter is elected president
		United States celebrates its bicentennial
1977	★	President Carter issues a pardon to Vietnam War draft evaders
		Jacqueline Onassis becomes an editor at Doubleday
1978	★	People's Republic of China and the United States begin full diplomatic ties
1979	★	Iranians seize U.S. Embassy in Tehran and hold American hostages
1980	★	Ronald Reagan is elected president
1981	★	Iranians release the U.S. hostages
		Sandra Day O'Connor becomes the first woman appointed to the Supreme Court
1983	★	Sally Ride becomes the first American woman astronaut in space
1984	★	Ronald Reagan is reelected president
1986	★	Space shuttle *Challenger* explodes, killing all on board
1987	★	United States and Soviet Union sign nuclear missile reduction treaty
1988	★	George Bush is elected president
1989	★	Berlin Wall comes down
1990	★	Iraq invades Kuwait
1991	★	United States leads allies in Persian Gulf War
		Iraq is pushed out of Kuwait
1992	★	Bill Clinton is elected president
1993	★	North American Free Trade Agreement is passed
1994	★	Richard M. Nixon dies on April 22
		Jacqueline Bouvier Kennedy Onassis dies on May 19

Fast Facts about Jacqueline Bouvier Kennedy Onassis

Born: July 28, 1929, in Southampton, New York

Died: May 19, 1994, in her Fifth Avenue apartment in New York City

Burial Site: Arlington National Cemetery in Virginia

Parents: John "Jack" Bouvier III and Janet Lee Bouvier

Education: Miss Chapin's School for Girls (New York City), Miss Porter's Finishing School (Farmington, Connecticut), Vassar College (Poughkeepsie, New York), Sorbonne University (Paris, France), George Washington University (Washington, D.C.)

Jobs and Careers: Inquiring reporter/photographer for the *Washington Times–Herald*, book editor at Viking and at Doubleday

Marriage: To John F. Kennedy on September 12, 1953, until his death on November 22, 1963; to Aristotle Onassis on October 20, 1968, until his death in March 1975

Children: Caroline Bouvier Kennedy, John F. Kennedy Jr., and Patrick Bouvier Kennedy (died two days after birth)

Places She Lived: Long Island and New York City (1929–1943), Washington, D.C. (1943–1944, 1951–1968), Connecticut (1944–1948), Poughkeepsie, New York (1948–1950), Paris, France (1950–1951), Greece and New York City (1968–1975), New York City (1975–1994); with summer homes in Newport, Rhode Island, and Hyannis Port, Massachusetts

Major Achievements:

* Restored the White House as a historical showcase for the country's heritage and gave a nationally televised guided tour of the restoration
* Invited world-famous musicians and actors to perform at the White House
* Helped raise funds for the National Cultural Center (now the Kennedy Center for the Performing Arts)
* Traveled widely throughout the world with the president and on her own
* Planned the dignified funeral of her husband, President John F. Kennedy
* Raised funds for and helped establish the John F. Kennedy Library
* Helped save important buildings in New York City from being demolished

Fast Facts about
John F. Kennedy's Presidency

Term of Office: Elected in 1960; served as the thirty-fifth president of the United States from 1961 until his death by assassination on November 22, 1963

Vice President: Lyndon Baines Johnson (1961–1963); Johnson became president of the United States when Kennedy died

Major Policy Decisions and Legislation:
* Issued an executive order that created the Peace Corps, March 1, 1961
* Backed the Bay of Pigs invasion of Cuba that ended in failure, April 17–20, 1961
* Signed the Alliance for Progress accord along with leaders from 19 Latin American nations, August 17, 1961
* Sent military advisers to South Vietnam, 1961
* Sent messages to Congress seeking federal aid to public education (1961, 1962), asking for a project to land on the moon (1961), proposing civil-rights legislation and medical care for the elderly (1963)
* Forced the Soviet Union to dismantle missile bases in Cuba, October 1962

Major Events:
* President Kennedy holds the first presidential press conference on live television, January 25, 1961.
* The first manned American spacecraft is launched, May 5, 1961.
* The Berlin Wall goes up, August 1961.
* President Kennedy appoints Byron White and Arthur Goldberg as associate justices of the U.S. Supreme Court (1962).
* The University of Mississippi is desegregated with help of federal troops, September 1962.
* The Twenty-fourth Amendment is added to the U.S. Constitution, which states that citizens' right to vote will not be denied if they have not paid a poll tax or any other tax.
* Civil-rights workers march on Washington, D.C., and Martin Luther King Jr. gives his "I Have a Dream" speech at the Lincoln Memorial, September 1963.

Where to Visit

The Capitol Building
Constitution Avenue
Washington, D.C. 20510
(202) 225-3121

John Fitzgerald Kennedy Library
Columbia Point
Boston, Massachusetts 02125
Phone: (617) 929-4500
Fax: (617) 929-4538

Museum of American History of the Smithsonian Institution
"First Ladies: Political and Public Image"
14th Street and Constitution Avenue, N.W.
Washington, D.C. 20560
(202) 357-2008

National Archives
Constitution Avenue
Washington, D.C. 20408
(202) 501-5000

White House
1600 Pennsylvania Avenue
Washington, D.C. 20500
Visitors Office: (202) 456-7041

White House Historical Association (WHHA)
740 Jackson Place NW
Washington, D. C. 20503
(202) 737-8292

Online Sites of Interest

The First Ladies of the United States of America

http://www2.whitehouse.gov/WH/glimpse/firstladies/html/firstladies.html

A portrait and biographical sketch of each First Lady plus links to other White House sites

History Happens

http://www.usahistory.com/presidents

A site that contains fast facts about John F. Kennedy, including personal information and term in office

Jacqueline Bouvier Kennedy: First Lady

http://www.cs.umb.edu/jfklibrary/jbkmenu.htm

A virtual museum exhibit of the John F. Kennedy Library; includes photos, an extensive biography of the First Lady, a description of the Kennedy wedding, a few photos from the exhibit including her wedding dress and engagement ring, information on the White House preser-vation and restoration project, and a link to the JFK Library home page

John F. Kennedy Library & Museum

http://www.swift-tourism.com/jfk.htm

A site that contains a description of the New Museum at the Kennedy Library; includes a few pictures

The White House

http://www.whitehouse.gov/WH/Welcome.html

Information about the current president and vice president; White House history and tours; biographies of past presidents and their families; a virtual tour of the historic building, current events; also includes a few pictures

The White House for Kids

http://www.whitehouse.gov/WH/kids/html/kidshome.html

Includes information about White House kids, past and present; famous "First Pets," past and present; historic moments of the presidency; and much more

For Further Reading

Anderson, Catherine Corley. *Jacqueline Kennedy Onassis: Woman of Courage*. Minneapolis: Lerner Publications Company, 1995.

Clinton, Susan M. *First Ladies*. Cornerstones of Freedom series. Chicago: Childrens Press, 1994.

Condon, Dianne Russell. *Jackie's Treasures: The Fabled Objects from the Auction of the Century*. New York: Clarkson Potter, 1996.

Devaney, John. *The Vietnam War*. New York: Franklin Watts, 1992.

Editors of *Life* magazine. *Remembering Jackie: A Life in Pictures*. New York: Warner Books, 1994.

Fisher, Leonard E. *The White House*. New York: Holiday House, 1989.

Gormley, Beatrice. *First Ladies*. New York: Scholastic, Inc., 1997.

Gould, Lewis L. (ed.). *American First Ladies: Their Lives and Their Legacy*. New York: Garland Publishing, 1996.

Gow, Catherine Hester. *The Cuban Missile Crisis*. World History series. San Diego: Lucent Books, 1997.

Guzzetti, Paula. *The White House*. Parsippany, N. J.: Silver Burdett Press, 1995.

Hawes, Esme. *The Life and Times of Jackie Onassis*. New York: Chelsea House Publishers, 1997.

Kent, Deborah. *The White House*. Chicago: Childrens Press, 1994.

Kent, Zachary. *John F. Kennedy: Thirty-Fifth President of the United States*. Encyclopedia of Presidents series. Chicago: Childrens Press, 1987.

Klapthor, Margaret Brown. *The First Ladies*. 8th edition. Washington, D.C.: White House Historical Association, 1995.

Mayo, Edith P. (ed.). *The Smithsonian Book of the First Ladies: Their Lives, Times, and Issues*. New York: Henry Holt, 1996.

Stein, R. Conrad. *The Assassination of John F. Kennedy*. Cornerstones of Freedom series. Chicago: Childrens Press, 1992.

Index

Page numbers in **boldface type** indicate illustrations

Photo Identifications

Cover: Photograph of Jacqueline Kennedy as First Lady
Page 8:   Jackie Kennedy, August 1963
Page 16:   Jacqueline Lee Bouvier at about age four
Page 28:   Jacqueline Bouvier as the *Washington Times–Herald* Inquiring Reporter
Page 38:   Official photograph of Jacqueline Bouvier Kennedy as First Lady
Page 50:   Official White House portrait of First Lady Jacqueline Kennedy
Page 68:   A close-up of Jackie, in mourning, taken the day before her husband's funeral
Page 78:   A May 1992 photograph of Jackie and her children, John Jr., and Caroline

Photo Credits©

Sygma— Stanley Tretick, cover

AP/Wide World Photos— 8, 11 (bottom), 12, 24 (top), 28, 32 (top), 41, 46, 49, 52 (top right), 54 (both pictures), 55, 62 (bottom), 64 (bottom left), 71 (top), 72, 76, 80, 84, 85 (top), 86, 90, 92, 93, 98 (bottom), 100 (bottom)

UPI/Corbis–Bettmann— 10, 11 (top), 14, 20 (top), 22, 33, 34 (both pictures), 35, 40 (both pictures), 43, 45 (top), 47, 48 (bottom), 52 (bottom right), 58 (bottom), 60, 65 (both pictures), 66 (both pictures), 68, 70, 71 (bottom), 73, 74, 77, 81 (bottom), 85 (bottom), 87, 89 (left), 99, 100 (top)

Corbis–Bettmann— 13, 15, 23, 42

John Fitzgerald Kennedy Library— 16, 18, 20 (bottom), 31, 36, 53, 56 (both pictures), 57, 61 (both pictures), 62 (top), 67, 98 (top); Miss Porter's School, 25, 26; Burchmann, 32 (bottom); White House/Mark Shaw, 38; USA Signal Corps, 48 (top)

Chapin School— 21

Miss Porter's School— 24 (bottom)

Vassar College Library— 27

Stock Montage, Inc.— 44, 45 (inset), 52 (top left and bottom left), 101; Reprinted with permission, The Chicago Sun–Times © 1996, 83

White House Historical Association— 50, 58 (top left and right)

SuperStock International, Inc.— Leon Dishman, 64 (top left); Mary Eleanor Browning, 64 (right); Eric Carle, 88

Reuters/Corbis–Bettmann— 78, 89 (right)

H. Armstrong Roberts— W. Metzen, 81 (top)

About the Author

Dan Santow is a former producer of *The Oprah Winfrey Show* and writer at *People* magazine. He is the author of *The Irreverent Guide: Chicago* (Frommer's/Macmillan, 1996) and has been published in many magazines, including *Redbook*, *Town & Country*, *Metropolitan Home*, *Men's Health*, *Chicago* magazine, the *Chicago Tribune Magazine*, and *Advertising Age*, among others. Mr. Santow is a graduate of Vassar College and holds a master's degree in journalism from Northwestern University. He lives in Chicago.